# 101 London Travel Tips

BY

Jonathan and Jacqueline Thomas

Anglotopia.net

# CONTENTS

# Welcome!
## About This Book

We think of London as our second home. The idea of this book came from various mishaps on the travels that we have had while exploring this great city.

We've traveled to London 10 times now and we've learned something new on every trip.

This book will help you easily navigate through London's quirks. Keep in mind that as you travel, you are, in fact, traveling. You have chosen a vacation to immerse yourself in a new culture. If you're open-minded and relaxed, you will have a wonderful time.

Tourists travel from around the globe to see the treasures that London holds. Make sure to get out and see the city. Take full advantage of all of the free attractions and fantastic parks. Take in a nice cup of tea at teatime or have a pint at a pub. Fully immerse yourself in the culture, and you will have a fabulous time. We promise.

London is a unique melting pot of cultures and people. You will encounter people from across the globe in London. Some are the nicest people on Earth and others leave something to be desired. Just be polite, and remember, a smile goes a long way.

Bon Voyage!

Jonathan and Jackie Thomas

# Chapter 1

# PLANNING YOUR TRIP

Planning ahead is the best way to make the most of your trip to London. The first section of this book will give you some tips on planning ahead to make the most of your trip to London with tips you won't find anywhere else.

## 1. Pack Light For London

By far the worst part of traveling to Britain is dealing with luggage. It's heavy and hard to get through airports, the Tube and around London's bumpy sidewalks. Now that airlines charge extra for heavier luggage and extra bags, it's just not worth the added cost and trouble.

Our travel philosophy is that less is more when it comes to packing for London.

You don't need to take as much with you as you think. London hotels are small and there won't be much room for massive luggage. Redefine what you think is essential when traveling, and try to keep everything down to one carry-on and one checked bag.

Pack simply, plan your outfits in advance, be willing to mix and match. Try to keep shoes to a minimum. We usually take one pair of good walking shoes and a pair of dressier shoes.

If you want to pack really light, don't be afraid to do a load of laundry during your trip. Most hotels have facilities and most neighborhoods have a laundromat. It's a great way to meet some locals.

## 2. Souvenirs

We understand the urge – the urge to snap up as many London-themed gifts as you can carry for everyone back home, especially if this is your first trip to London. There will not be a shortage of souvenir shops to tempt you into parting with your cash.

Pretty much every souvenir store in central London has all the same tatty crap. Most of it is made in China (not in Britain). Most of it is not that special.

We recommend shopping for quality, not quantity. Sure, you need to pick up some postcards and what not, but focus instead on getting unique gifts that you won't be able to get anywhere else – gifts that will sit on a shelf and be admired or have a good story. That can mean good finds in a market or antique store.

If you really want some tatty souvenirs then save your souvenir shopping for the airport. There are ample stores there where you can buy all that neat stuff tax-free instead.

## 3. Grocery Shopping/Snacking

Every neighborhood in London has a corner shop or chain grocery store, and if you want to save a ton of money on eating, then we recommend stopping in on your first day in London.

Going to a grocery store and stocking up on snacks will save you a lot of money on meals, especially if you plan picnics. It's a great way to save money on food, which will be your biggest cost while in London.

Stores like Marks & Spencer have daily deals where you can get an entire meal for two for just £10, including entree, dessert and wine. It's a great deal for tasty food. You'll pay more at stores like Harrods, Waitrose, etc.

Breakfast is the most important meal of the day, so we always stock up breakfast foods like muffins, fruits, and cereal. That way we get a good breakfast in the room, and when we leave the hotel we're fueled up for a full day of London sightseeing.

## 4. Dealing with the Rain

Despite the popular myth, it doesn't rain ALL the time in London. In fact, most of the year, London has pretty fair weather. Believe it or not, in 2012, London is under drought conditions! However, it COULD rain at any time, so carry a small umbrella with you. You won't look stupid.

## 5. Clothing Size Conversion

Most clothing and shoe sizes will have the equivalent US size on the labels. As a general guide, women's jeans/denim waist sizing is the same for the US and the UK. Letter sizing (e.g. S, M, L, XL) is also the same for the US and UK. For example a US size S (small) is the same as a UK size S.

UK and the US men's clothing share the same clothing sizes for both casual and formal wear. This includes neck size, sleeve length, sport coat/jacket sizing (also called chest size), and waist size.

Men's and women's shoe sizes are different in the US and UK. Measure your feet and try different sizes on to ensure a proper fit.

## 6. 24-Hour Time

Like the rest of Europe, the British use the 24-hour clock (aka military time) and the 12-hour clock interchangeably.

Often you'll find TV and theatre show times quoted in 12-hour time, while trains and bus scheduled will be in 24-hour time. This inevitably leads to confusion amongst travelers in London.

The solution is simple. The easiest way to translate the different clocks is this: subtract 12 from whatever the 24-hour time is. For example 23:00 = 11:00pm.

## 7. Euros

The British are very proud of their currency, the pound sterling, and have no intentions to give it up for the euro, especially in light of recent economic troubles in Europe.

That said, many stores in central London will actually take Euros, and most items have the price in euros on them. However, not all stores do this, and you may not get the best exchange rate this way.

Many stores will also process the credit card transaction in pounds or euros (and sometimes dollars). Keep in mind, though, that this is just another way for the store to make more money, and you're not guaranteed to get the best exchange rate by doing this. When in doubt, pay in pounds, whether you pay in cash or swipe.

## 8. Top 5 London iPhone Apps

Here is our selection of iPhone apps that you can't live without when traveling to London.

**London Tube** - The standard map for the London underground also features a guide to each line, stations, a route planner, and it will also locate you with GPS and tell you the closest Tube station.

**Mini A to Z London** - There are several A-Z apps for London, but the mini one is suitable for tourists and features a map of central London with all the major attractions. It works offline, and will also use GPS to locate you to help guide you on your way. It's also fun to look at.

**Lonely Planet London Guide** – This is our favorite of the London guidebooks that have been converted for the iPhone. It features plenty of offline information, maps, and everything you need to enjoy your trip in London. It also has a very nice interface.

**Time Out London** - This free app from Time Out will keep you up to date with all the latest happenings and events in London.

**WiFi Free United Kingdom** - This invaluable little app shows you where the nearest free wireless Internet is. As it's hard to fine in London, this app is a must. Click to download.

## 9. Top 5 London Guide Books

While the iPhone is a great tool for planning your trip to London, there's still nothing like opening the pages of a good guidebook and planning out your trip.

**Rick Steves' London** - The standard bearer for planning a trip to London, Rick's books are accessible, easy to read, and feature a ton of great information. Do not go to London without it. Click for more info.

**DK Eyewitness London** - This book is more useful for its treasure trove of pictures rather than up-to-date tourist information. But it serves a purpose in making London recognizable and putting key places on the map (something the Rick Steves' book shuns). Click for more info.

**Tired of London, Tired of Life** - A new guidebook to London that features something new to do every day of the year. It's filled with unique experiences, many of which you wouldn't normally find in a London guidebook. Click for more info.

**24 Hours in London** - Another guidebook with an interesting twist, instead of listing a bunch of things to do, this book lists cool things to do throughout the day based on the time. It's a very cool way to find new and interesting experiences. Click for more info.

**Secret London** - This is not really a guidebook but more of a peek into the sites of London that tourists don't normally see. It features tons of interesting information as well as guided walks if you're an intrepid explorer. Click for more info.

## 10. Pack Your New British Umbrella in Your Luggage or Ship it Home

The British make beautiful umbrellas – way better than anything you'll find in the States. Our umbrellas are usually made of plastic, and won't survive a good gust of wind. Being from windy Chicago, this is a problem for us.

Several trips ago, we picked up the perfect British umbrella in a small shop. It's black, long, and looks exactly like you'd expect an umbrella from London to look.

Because it wouldn't fit in our already full luggage, we decided to just carry it on the plane with us.

They wouldn't let us take it through security. Apparently an umbrella is too much like a weapon (it has a metal point). Thankfully, we were able to check the umbrella, and it arrived at our destination unharmed. Lesson is, if you plan to buy a fancy umbrella, have it shipped home or make sure your luggage will be big enough to carry it.

## 11. Outlet Converters

We made the mistake of splashing out on an expensive voltage converter on one of our first trips to London. You generally don't need a voltage converter, though, just a plug adapter. Most American appliances and electronics convert voltage on their own.

You can pick up plug converters pretty cheap at most stores like Target or Walmart. Many come with a kit that has many. It's best for have 3 or 4 with you so you won't have to ration your electronic device charging.

Apple also makes a plug adapter kit that has the UK adapter in it as well. If you use Apple products, then it's definitely worth picking up. It will work with all of them, and it only costs $40.

## 12. Limited Trading Hours on Sundays

Britain is not quite a 24-hour society like the USA. This is slowly changing, but you will be very surprised to see when things actually close. Many places in London are closed on Sundays or have different operating hours, including museums and stores.

Retail stores are usually open only 6 hours on Sundays (10am to 4pm typically), so it's important to check ahead before setting out. We once planned to go to Harrods on the last Sunday of one of our trips. We went all the way there to find that the doors were locked, because they were closed on Sundays. We missed our chance as we had a flight to catch. Harrods is now open on Sundays, but it's always a good idea to check operating hours before heading to a destination.

## 13. Six Fun Things to Do at Night in London

Looking for some fun things to do on a night out in London? Often we're so exhausted after a day of sightseeing in London that all we want to do is order in for dinner and watch British telly. But how often are you in London? If after a rest you can muster some more energy, here are a few ideas for things you can do.

**Leicester Square** - The center of London's entertainment scene, there's plenty to eat, movie theatres, casinos, adult stores and much more. Something for everyone.

**See a Musical** - You really can't go all the way to London without seeing a West End Musical. Les Mis is one of our favorites.

**Go to the movies** - A movie is a fun thing to do, and won't break the bank. Try to see something you can't just see back home. You didn't go all the way to London to see a movie you can see at your local multiplex. One difference, though: you'll notice you have to pick your seat when you buy your ticket, and that's where you have to sit!

**Eat a fancy dinner** - Save a little of your trip budget to eat at some of London's nicer restaurants. There are plenty in Covent Garden and the area around there. Our favorite is Gordon Ramsay's Maze Grill on Grosvenor Square. Most expensive meal we ever had, but it was by far the best.

**Walk along the Southbank** - The Southbank (which means the southside of the Thames) is home to a vibrant arts and dining scene. You'll also enjoy great views of London lit up in the night.

**London Eye Night Flight** - The London Eye at night is an amazing experience as you get to see the Capital lit up in all its glory. Book ahead, and if you have budget to spare, book a champagne flight.

## 14. Get a Hotel Close to the Tube

You will likely be spending a lot of time on the Tube as it's the easiest and cheapest way to get around Central London. Make sure that you don't spend a lot of time walking to the nearest Tube Station. It's no big deal in the morning when you're ready to see London, but at the end of the day it can feel like the Bataan death march if your hotel is far from the Tube.

When booking your hotel, check Google Maps and make sure it's near a Tube Stop. Most hotel websites will also show how close they are, but be careful – many just say the distance, but that doesn't mean anything on London's spaghetti streets. There's nothing worse than a 1-mile walk going in circles on London's confusing streets at the end of the day after you're exhausted from seeing the sites.

## 15. Five Things to Do in Notting Hill

Notting Hill has been made famous by the film of the same name, which has been a blessing and a curse for the area. Here's our list of five things to do in the neighborhood.

**The Market** - While it's very crowded on Saturdays, definitely pay a visit to the Portobello Road Market.

**Hummingbird Bakery** – American-style baked treats that are better than you can get back home.

**Eat a Meal** - Notting Hill has a world-class selection of restaurants.

**Museum of Brands, Packaging and Advertising** - A neat little niche museum on an interesting topic (to us at least).

**Queens Ice and Bowl** - London's year-round ice skating rink.

## 16. Five Things to Do in Islington

Islington is a residential area popular with young Londoners, and the neighborhood has a great vibe to it. Here's our list of a few cool things to do in Islington.

**Football** - Take in a Football match at Emirates Stadium.

**Le Mercury** - The best French food in the heart of London.

**Breakfast Club** - An 80s-themed breakfast joint that will feel like home to Americans, especially those from Chicago (John Hughes theme).

**Highbury Fields** - It's not Hyde Park, but this local park is green, open, and beautiful.

**Screen on the Green** - A beautiful old Art-Deco movie theater.

# Chapter 2

# CULTURAL

This chapter will guide you through the cultural landscape of modern day London. London culture is hard to define, and there are many types. But there are a few things you can learn to help you fit in better.

## 17. Tipping in London

This is a complicated topic but we'll try to address it as simply as possible. Generally, you don't need to tip in London. This is because most restaurants have a service charge tacked on the bill that is essentially a mandatory tip.

It's been our experience that service is pretty bad in London – even in the nicer restaurants – so most of the time a tip isn't even deserved. If you receive particularly good service, then by all means tip. But check the bill first and make sure there's not a service charge so you don't pay twice.

Services are a little different. In a Black London Cab, for example, it's a common courtesy to round up to the next pound when paying. If you receive some other sort of service and are happy with the service given, then no one will be unhappy with a tip.

Don't feel obligated to tip, though, especially if you receive bad service.

## 18. Stand on the Right

This may seem minor, but on escalators and similar situations, stand on the right so people can pass you. There will be signs to remind you. Pay attention so no one runs into you or is forced to say "excuse me, love."

This is a huge source of frustration for Londoners as they navigate tourists on the network. This rule works for sidewalks as well - just try to stay out of the way.

## 19. Look Right!

Traffic in Britain generally comes from the right - not the left as it does in the USA. It's important to remember this when crossing any street.

Really, you should always look both ways, but it's important to train your mind to check the right. There are also a lot of one-way streets in London where you would do well to look left.

If you forget, generally there will be writing on the street crossing that will tell you to look right, but you can't always rely on this.

## 20. Queue Up

It is often joked that queuing up (or standing in line to the rest of us) is a cherished national pastime in Britain. They do take it very seriously.

In the USA, when there's a line for something, unless directed by a higher authority, there will be chaos as people cut in and attempt to get to the front first. In Britain, the British line up automatically without direction and maintain the integrity of the line (no cutting!).

Queuing also creates situations where you'll have time chat with Brits. It's a good way to make a "line friend," but don't expect it to go beyond that. Safe topics to talk about include the weather, the weather, and the weather.

As an American you'll just have to learn to stand in line and be patient about it. It bears repeating: do not, under any circumstance, jump the queue. Brits hold a grudge for life.

## 21. Navigating the London Pub

The pub is the central part of British cultural life and you would be remiss to skip it on a trip to London. Most neighborhoods have a pub that's a good place to relax, meet locals, get a good meal, and become a temporary local.

Here are a few tips so you don't look like a pillock (that's idiot in American speak).

Go to the bar to order food and drinks. Most pubs won't have wait service.

Order beer by the pint or half-pint

You aren't obligated to tip in a pub.

Don't be horrified if you see a child in a pub, it's normal to the Brits.

If you go with a group, it's common for each person in the group to take orders and buy the rounds.

## 22. Londoners are not Americans

Londoners are not like Americans – they are a breed unto themselves. You wouldn't expect a Londoner to be like someone from your local town, would you?

They do things differently – sometimes VERY differently. This will seem alien to you, but it's very normal to them.

You're there to learn, observe and enjoy yourself (never to judge). The sooner you lose the expectation that a Londoner will treat you like a fellow American would, the sooner you'll enjoy your trip.

## 23. Soho Sex Language

Soho is the "red light district"of London. It's slowly being taken over by fancy restaurants and shops, but it still has a dented reputation. This area is best avoided at night, as that's when the prostitutes (and the elements that come with them) are out in full force.

Prostitution is not illegal in Britain. However, streetwalkers are illegal (and so is purchasing the services of one). Just walking down the street in Soho, you will have scantily clad women heckle you and attempt to pull you into the various clubs.

Here is some interesting vocabulary to help you navigate the area.

Models = Prostitute (you will see lots of signs saying, "model." This means there's a prostitute waiting in a flat up the stairs to offer her services).

Prozzy = Prostitute

Clip Joint = Bar where they lure you in with the prospect of "live girls," and then rip you off and threaten your safety if you don't pay up.

Peep Show = Pay £2, and you get to watch a woman dance around naked in a room for 2 minutes.

## 24. Chuggers

A chugger is someone you won't be able to avoid on London's street – especially in busy tourist areas. Slang for "charity muggers," they're people who work on commission for charities.

They accost you on the sidewalk and ask you to donate to their cause. While this sounds rather nice, they actually pocket a percentage as their earnings.

They are annoying and can be very aggressive as they are just trying to make some money under the guise of supporting a good cause. You will not offend them by ignoring them.

## 25. Don't Bring up the War - or Claim America Saved their Asses

This may seem like common sense to most, but don't ever bring up World War II in casual conversation. It's a political minefield.

The British are extremely proud of their wartime history, and contrary to popular myth, they suffered a great deal and for quite a bit longer until we bothered to get involved (and will not hesitate to mention this to you).

We did not "save their asses in the war," so don't even think of saying that. If you think this never happens, it does. We've seen it ourselves.

## 26. The Customer is not Always Right in London

The British have a far different conception of customer service than the USA. Always be prepared for poor customer service – especially on the railroads. While most Americans default to verbally assaulting ineffective customer service, avoid doing it in Britain. It will get you nowhere.

Expect poor customer service everywhere, and when you get GOOD customer service, it will come off as a bit of a treat. Service is the worst in London's restaurants – even the nice ones.

## 27.Useful London Slang

One thing you'll notice when you travel to London is all the strange words they use to describe things. Sometimes they make sense, sometimes they don't. To help the wayward tourist, here's a list of words you'll here when you travel to London.

- **Tube** = London Underground Network

- **The Knowledge** = Geographical information London's black cab drivers have to learn to be licensed. They have to learn every street in London.

- **Boris Bus** = Boris Johnson's key platform of replacing the old London Routemaster bus.

- **Red Ken** = The name of London's former Mayor Ken Livingston who leaned VERY far to the left.

- **The Standard** = What some call the Evening Standard – the evening paper dedicated to London.

- **The City** = The City of London – the square mile bit of central London that goes back 2 thousand years.

- **Square Mile** = Also the City of London.

- **Congestion Charge** = Tax on all cars entering the central London congestion charge zone.

- **Silicon Roundabout** = Area around Old Street that's a hub for new media and tech companies.

- **Council Estate** = Public housing

- **The Blitz** = Period in 1940 when London was bombed by the Nazis.

- **M25** = The Orbital Highway that encircles London.

- **Westway** = Elevated Highway in West London.

- **Mind the Gap** = Watch your step when stepping from a train to a platform.

- **Buck House** = Buckingham Palace

- **The Tower** = Tower of London

- **A-Z** = A popular London map guide that's indispensable to locals and long-term visitors (Extra note – Londoners will say "A to Zed").

- **GMT** = Greenwich Mean Time.

- **Cockney** = Someone born within earshot of the bells of St Mary-le-Bow.

- **Offy** = Convenience Store.

- **Off License** = Convenience Store.

- **Take Away** = Cheap to-go food.

- **Crossrail** = New cross-London underground railway line currently under construction.

- **Bobby** = London policeman.

- **Zebra Crossing** = Pedestrian crossing.

- **Home Counties** = Generic name for the counties around London: Bedfordshire, Berkshire, Buckinghamshire, Cambridgeshire, Dorset, Essex, Hampshire, Hertfordshire,

Kent, Middlesex, Oxfordshire, Surrey and Sussex.

- **Pissed** = Drunk.
- **Pants** = Underwear or something that sucks.
- **Trousers** = Pants.
- **Quid** = Pound.
- **Knackered** = Tired.
- **Loo** = Toilet.
- **Kip** = Sleep/Nap.
- **Tenner** = £10.

## 28. Muslim Population

London is an incredibly diverse city, so be prepared to see Muslims pretty much everywhere. You will come across many women in burkas.

It can be unsettling to Americans, but try to understand that Britain is a free country, and the women do it by choice. The sooner you understand that diversity is good, the better time you'll have in London.

British Muslims are just trying to get on with their daily lives, just as you are. Just because they look different or have different beliefs does not automatically make them dangerous. There are some that have trouble integrating with British society, but they are the exception, not the rule.

## 29. "Special Relationship" isn't Very Special in Practical Reality

Don't expect special treatment because you're an American or because we "saved them in the war." To the British, you're just like every other foreign invader – you're just more cheerful, louder and speak a similar language.

The biggest wakeup call you'll get when you leave the US for the first time is when you have to get in line at Heathrow for customs with everyone else in the world while the British sail through the Citizen line. As Americans, we have no special rights in the UK other than that we can travel there for up to 6 months without a visa.

## 30. London is a Global City

London is a truly global city, and it's possible to get through the whole day without actually encountering any Brits at all.

Because of this, many people perceive London to be a rather rude city because it's full of foreigners. It is. Be prepared for it. Most restaurants have foreign waiters and waitresses, and it can be hard to communicate, but you'll just have to get used to it. Be kind and patient.

## 31. Leicester Square

It's pronounced Lester Square. Also, Grosvenor Square is pronounced Grove-ner Square.

## 32. Quiet Down!

When Londoners were recently surveyed about American tourists, the top annoyance on their list of complaints was that Americans are LOUD.

While it may be hard for Americans to stomach, we are indeed very loud, especially when we're traveling abroad.

The British are a quiet and reserved people (almost to a fault). And while they'll give you the benefit of the doubt if you speak too loudly (you don't know any better), try to bring your voice down a few notches while you're in London. Don't worry; people will still be able to hear you.

## 33. Five Things to Do in the West End

London's West End area is its most vibrant and tourist friendly. Here's our list of five things you should do when you're in the area.

**Take in a show** - Les Mis is one of our favorites, though not very British in subject matter!

**Stroll though Covent Garden** - Lots of wonderful shops and a beautiful piazza.

**Eat a Meal in Leicester Square** - Plenty of tourist-themed fine dining in the area.

**Visit the National Gallery** – World-class art in a beautiful setting.

**People watch in Trafalgar Square** - Best place to watch people in London.

## 34. Five Things to Do in Knightsbridge

Knightsbridge has a reputation as a very wealthy area, but it's also filled with many culturally rich attractions. Here's our selection of five things you can do in the area.

**Harrods** - You cannot go to London without going there.

**Hyde Park** - Our favorite London park has so much to see and do.

**Victoria & Albert Museum** - An eclectic mix of many subjects in a beautiful setting.

**Science Museum** - Dedicated to Science. Don't miss the Darwin Centre.

**Harvey Nichols** - The OTHER department store in Knightsbridge.

# Chapter 3

# LODGING

After your airfare to London, your hotel or lodging will be your next most expensive cost. Budget hotels can be a nightmare, and they usually don't meet American standards. Here's our selection of tips to make the most of your lodging.

## 35. Is it Hot in Here?

Despite London being a modern First World country, you will be surprised to find that most hotels and businesses don't actually have air conditioning. This is hard to get used to in London.

Generally, you don't need air conditioning, because London stays moderately cool most of the year. There are a couple months in the summer, though, where things get hot.

It's not so much that it gets sweltering – temperatures above 85 degrees are pretty uncommon. It's just that you never have a chance to cool off, so it feels hotter than it actually is.

The Tube gets oppressively hot as most of it is not air conditioned, and masses of people create an astounding amount of heat.

Carry a bottle of water with you, and try to avoid the Tube in July and August. Thankfully, most new hotels have air conditioning, so if your budget allows you to stay somewhere newer, you'll be able to cool off.

## 36. Hotel Rooms are Small. Deal with it.

Unless you can afford to spend $500+ a night, your hotel room will be small and not up to the standards you'd expect from a Holiday Inn in America.

This is pretty much the way it is in London. Budget hotels feature small rooms, windows without a view (unless a concrete courtyard is a view), musty furnishings, and sometimes tiny TVs. Staff will generally be unhelpful (and Eastern European). They'll also be rather noisy (especially during the breakfast rush).

Don't be sold on a hotel based on "free continental breakfast." This will most likely be food you won't want to eat or all the good food will be gone before you get down there. It's usually a buffet featuring soggy eggs and toast. It's not worth paying extra for it.

We're rather prosaic about hotels. We just think of it as a place to lay our heads at night. You don't need an excuse to stay in your room anyway. A crappy hotel gives you an excuse to spend as much time out in London as possible.

## 37. Hotel Check-in Time is Pretty Ironclad

Many of the flights from the USA land in the early London morning, some as early as 6 am. While this is kind of nice as you have the whole day ahead of you, it's usually not since you can't check into most hotels until after 3 in the afternoon.

Some will let you check in early, but more often than not, you'll be sitting around their lobby for a few hours waiting to check-in. If you're staying at a good hotel, you can check your bags with the concierge, and then go out and explore for the day before checking into your room at the proper time (but take your passport and valuables with you).

Also, many of the cheaper touristy hotels cater to package tours, and the busloads of tourists usually arrive right at check-in time, so get your place in line first or else you'll find yourself in line with a bunch of grumpy Germans.

We recommend dropping off your bags and then eating a good breakfast/lunch – this will help reset your body clock.

## 38. Beware of Bed Bugs

The creepy crawlies have made a comeback in London, and we've seen some real horror stories from our readers and friends.

If you're not familiar with bed bugs, they're bugs that live in mattresses. They like to come out at night and bite unsuspecting blood donors. Their bites irritate the skin and often they're bad enough to require some sort of medical intervention.

Always check your mattress for bed bugs before settling in. They like to hide behind the mattress against the wall and in between the mattress, box spring, and the mattress seams. Don't be afraid to move things around and see.

If you spot a bedbug, immediately pick up your bags and get out of the room before they infest your bags, and you bring them home.

This tip even goes for nice hotels. Cleaner, nicer hotels are not immune to the creepy crawlies! We also recommend checking TripAdvisor before you book to make sure there haven't been any bed bug attacks lately. Reviewers will often report this (with gruesome pictures).

## 39. Self-Catering Flats are a Better Option for Families

Self-catering flats are a great way to live like a temporary local and experience living in London (something that's increasingly hard for Americans to do). However, renting a flat can be a little pricier than staying in a hotel.

If you're traveling in a group, renting a flat is the best option, as flats are well suited to families. You can get more than one bedroom for increased privacy and get full cooking facilities. You can save money on food by eating in.

The company London Connection (Click for Website) is a good place to start. It's run by Americans who own a ton of flats in London, and we like working with them. You can also check AirBNB.com – a site that lets people let out their spare rooms and flats to travelers.

## 40. Five Things to Do in St. James

St. James is a very genteel part of central London that has long associated with royalty and the upper classes. It's one of our favorite areas. Here are a few things you can do in the neighborhood.

**Fortnum & Mason** - An elegant and famous department store famous for their hampers of British goods.

**Piccadilly Arcade** - A charming and old covered street featuring many fancy shops.

**St James Palace** - It's not open to the public, but you can still admire its beauty and spot the odd British soldier guarding its safety.

**Lock & Company Hatters** - One of the oldest hat makers in London with prices to match their pedigree.

**Green Park** - Another stunning park not to be missed.

## 41. Five Things to Do in Kensington

South Kensington is one of our favorite areas of London (we've stayed there more than anywhere else). Here are our favorite things to do in the area.

**Kensington Palace** - The former home to Princess Diana recently went through a multi-million pound renovation.

**Holland Park** - Another beautiful London park. One cool thing to do is take in a performance at the Open Air Theatre.

**Shop on Kensington High Street** - Find some of the world's most famous brands here.

**Leighton House Museum** - Stunning stately home that's recently been restored to its former glory.

**The Orangery** - Located near Kensington Palace, this stunning restaurant is perfect for High Tea.

# Chapter 4

# FOOD

London has a huge variety of food, and if you're not careful, you'll spend a lot of money on your trip just eating to sustain yourself. Using these tips, you can offset that cost while still enjoying the best food London has to offer.

## 42. Familiar Foods/Differences

The biggest shock to your system in London will be the differences in food. If you have sensitive digestion (like we do), your body will need time to adjust to the differences in food. While a meal may look or seem like the same thing you'd eat back home, it will be different. All food in Britain is slightly different.

Pancakes are more like Crepes than American pancakes. They like to put crap in their hamburgers makes them closer resemble meatloaf. They use different frying oils, so fried things have a different taste. Cuts of steak are similar, however the filet steak is a comparable to a flat iron steak in the US.

Burger King is better than McDonald's in the UK and tastes closer to home. Even if the food sounds familiar, always be prepared for it to taste different. Always read the menu carefully, and don't assume just because it has the same name that it's the same thing.

## 43. Avoid Pizza Huts, Pizza Expresses, and Other Chain Restaurants

Their food sucks, and the service is generally horrible. We've not had many good experiences with the major chain restaurants (British and American).

Our stance is that you don't go all the way to Britain to have McDonalds, so why eat it?

The British chain restaurants are easy to spot in central London, as you'll see them all over the place. You can't spit without hitting a Garfunkel's or Aberdeen Steak House.

Look out for smaller cafes and mom and pop shops. They'll have the cheapest and tastiest food. Chain restaurants are geared toward tourists and have prices to match.

## 44. McDonald's is Different

If you're looking for a respite from British cooking and think that you can relax with a Big Mac, keep in mind that it tastes completely different than it does in the US. They use REAL beef in their burgers and the oils they use on the fries are different, giving everything a strange - yet better - taste.

Also, they don't really do breakfast at the McDonald's in the UK. I've searched in vain for hotcakes, but you'll never find them. One thing they do have (which the American ones should have) is donuts, which are rather tasty.

You also always have to ask for ketchup. It won't be out for you to help yourself.

## 45. Proper Fish and Chips

Proper fish and chips are comprised of one slab of breaded and fried fish (usually Cod), a side of chips, and mushy peas. You have never had authentic fish and chips outside of Britain. Most places in America get it wrong and serve fried strips of fish. In reality it's a slab of fish that's very challenging to eat with a knife and fork. Also of note is that the British eat with the fork tines DOWN when eating, and they don't switch hands like Americans do.

They're served properly with a tarter sauce, but no one will look down on you if you ask for ketchup. Chunky chips with fish and chips are a highlight of any London trip.

## 46. Don't Try to Bring Food Home

There's so much good food in London, but don't try to bring it home to the USA. We tried in the past, and it's almost always confiscated by US Customs and destroyed.

The only foods that you can bring back into the USA are things that are packaged and sealed. Even then, they might give you a hard time.

When in doubt, ask if the store can ship to the USA. If they tell you they can't, you most likely won't be able to bring it home.

## 47. Cookies!

We love a nice cookie, and we highly recommend Ben's Cookies. They have a location in Covent Garden as well as several more around central London.

We highly recommend the double chocolate cookies. They're so good, it's the first place we go when we get off the plane!

## 48. Cupcakes!

For the best cupcakes in the world, stop by the Hummingbird Bakery in Notting Hill on Portobello Road, home to a bakery that specializes in American-style baked goods.

They have all kinds of baked goods, but their cupcakes are the best in London. So good, they've now got multiple locations all over central London.

# Chapter 5

# ATTRACTIONS & DEALS

This is why you've come to London! Many of the major tourist attractions are pretty expensive, but using these tips you can make the most of your time in London and make sure you see everything you want to see!

## 49. Best Places to Hear Free Music

London has many places where you can hear great music for free. Here's a quick list of five places you can hear free music while in London.

- St Martin in the Field's at lunchtime every day.

- Covent Garden Market on the lower levels.

- Buskers on the South Bank of the River.

- Southbank Centre - free music often.

- St. James Church in Piccadilly. Free music recitals at 1:10 pm on Mondays, Wednesdays, and Fridays.

## 50. Buckingham Palace Opening

Buckingham Palace is one of the most popular tourist attractions in London, but most people don't know that it's only open to tours in August and September when the Queen is not in residence.

If you're in town during this time, it's well worth checking out. If you still want to tour one of the Queen's residences, check out Windsor Castle instead, which is a short train ride from central London. It has it's own set of grand rooms, beautiful artwork, and it's open year-round. Windsor Castle even has its own changing of the guard.

## 51. Changing of the Guard

The daily changing of the guard is one of the most popular must-sees on the tourist trail in London. It's worth seeing if you're interested in British Ceremonial Traditions (if you're not, don't bother).

The Changing of the Guard outside Buckingham Palace takes place daily throughout the summer months at 11:30 am. Outside of the summer months, it takes place every other day.

Be sure to confirm with the Changing of the Guard website for precise dates.

Arrive about 30-60 minutes in advance so you can stake out a good spot near the fence, otherwise you'll be craning your neck. It's also fun to watch from the Victoria Monument across from the palace.

## 52. Touring Parliament

Parliament is only open to the public for tours one day a week (Saturday), and when Parliament is not in session during the summer months.

You have to book tickets ahead in advance through Ticketmaster, and tickets cost £15 for adults (about $25). Tours depart every 15 minutes and last 75 minutes. On the tour you'll get to see the House of Commons and Lords Chambers, the Queen's Robing Room, the Royal Gallery, and Westminster Hall.

Security is tight and you're not allowed to take pictures except in Westminster Hall. See the website for booking information. Check ahead before planning on going.

## 53. Cheap Bus Tour of Central London

Most of the classic London Double Decker Routemasters have been taken out of service, but they still run them on two bus lines in Central London: Routes 9 and 15.

It's really affordable and fun to hop on, climb to the top, and ride the bus as it circles through all the London sites. It's also much less expensive than other bus "tours."

## 54. Is the Tate Modern Worth a Visit?

While the building is very cool and worth a visit for that, the Tate Modern is very overrated unless you're really into modern art, which most people aren't. The gift shop is insanely expensive. I go just to admire the building and the massive turbine hall.

The museum is free to enter, and they do have a few famous pieces of art including some Monets and a Jackson Pollack.

## 55. Speaker's Corner

This famous area in Hyde Park is considered the home of free speech where you are welcome to speak about anything you wish as long as you don't cause a riot.

It's colorful, fun and enlightening. You'll probably find speakers any day of the week, but Sunday is the best day to go. Some of the people speaking will be, shall we say, rather unconventional.

## 56. Top Five London Parks

London has some of the most beautiful parks in the world, and they're definitely worth a visit. You can relax for free and enjoy a picnic while mingling with locals.

**Hyde Park/Kensington Gardens** - This is a must visit. Check out the Serpentine Gallery, the paddle boats, the Princess Diana memorial and much more. In the winter they usually have a Christmas carnival.

**Regent's Park** - A huge park to spend some time in, also home to the residence of the US Ambassador and the London Zoo.

**St James Park** - Don't miss the great views of Buckingham Palace from the bridge on the Lake.

**Green Park** - Great place to have a rest under some beautiful trees.

**Hampstead Heath** - Don't miss the great views of the London skyline from the Parliament Hill.

## 57. 5 Must See London shows

You can't go to London without taking in a West End Show. Here are five classic shows that we recommend (and you should be able to get cheap tickets, too).

1. Wicked

2. Mamma Mia

3. Lion King

4. Les Miserables

5. Phantom of the Opera

## 58. Queensway

Queensway is not well known on the tourist track as it's primarily a residential area, but outside the Queensway Tube Stop and north up the street are lots of interesting places to shop and eat. There are a lot of local places you won't find anywhere else.

The street contains many restaurants (particularly Chinese, Arab and Mediterranean ones), pubs, letting agents, and high street stores. Near the northern end of the street is the multi-storey Whiteleys Shopping Centre, on the site of London's first department store, opened by William Whiteley in 1867. It's now a type of mall with lots of great shops (including a nice bookstore).

There's also an interesting maze-like shopping mall that's reminiscent of a Middle Eastern souk. It's a fun night out.

## 59. St. Martin in the Fields Concerts

This small church located right of Trafalgar square is also a center of classical music in London. They have free concerts during the lunch period, and they have regular evening concerts – which are amazing – in the very old church that was recently renovated. The concerts are affordable as well, so it you're on a budget and want some culture, it's the way to go.

After a concert, stroll through Trafalgar Square and then north to Leicester Square for a late dinner. It's a perfect London night out.

## 60. Five American Themed Places to Visit

You may come to London to see Britain, but there are a few bits of America in London that are a fun visit when you're in town.

**Roosevelt Statue** - Statue dedicated to Britain's wartime ally Franklin Roosevelt.

**Franklin House** - Ben Franklin's personal home during his time in London, recently restored to look exactly as it did when he lived there.

**Ed's Easy Diner** - An American style-diner located in London.

**US Embassy** - You can't really go inside and visit, but it's still an impressive building and an American Embassy has been in Grosvenor Square for as long as America has existed.

**American Memorial Chapel at St Paul's** - The American Memorial Chapel commemorates those Americans based in Britain who gave their lives in the Second World War.

## 61. Red Phone Boxes

You'll see the iconic red phone box everywhere, but they're also getting harder to find as they get replaced by new models and mobile phones. They are pretty easy to locate in the tourist areas.

It's always great fun to place a call home from there, and it's pretty convenient as you can swipe your credit card. Also, don't be surprised to see cards hanging in the phone booths for prostitutes. Some people collect them. But you may want to find a phone booth without them if your kids want a picture in a red phone box.

## 62. See London's Cathedrals for Free

Most Cathedrals in London will have a Choral Evensong service that's free for the public to attend. It's a great way to hear some beautiful music in a stunning setting for free.

After they close the Cathedrals to tourists, you can still come in and see the nightly service, usually held around 5 pm, for free.

You won't be able to enjoy the touristy bits as they will be closed off, but you still get to experience the amazing spaces.

## 63. Six London Museums you probably haven't heard of

London is home to a wide array of small museums that focus on some rather interesting subjects. Here's our selection of those worth a visit.

**The Cartoon Museum** - Dedicated to art behind political cartoons and comics.

**Hunterian Museum** - Dedicated to animal specimens.

**The Fan Museum** - Dedicated to fans! The kind you wave to stay cool.

**Sir John Soane's Museum** - Dedicated to the history of design and architecture.

**Bank of England Museum** - Learn the history of money.

**Museum of Brands and Packaging in Notting Hill** - Dedicated to the history of advertising and branding.

## 64. Straddle the Globe

You can stand in two different hemispheres at the Prime Meridian located at the Royal Observatory in Greenwich courtyard.

Sadly, this attraction is no longer free as you have to pay admission to the observatory now. But the observatory is worth a visit on its own, so we highly recommend it.

## 65. Best Place for People Watching

If you want to just sit around and watch London go by, grab a sandwich and sit on the steps to the National Gallery in Trafalgar Square for some of the finest people watching in London. Check out Hyde Park as well for great people watching.

## 66. Zoo Life in London

There are two world-class zoos in London: The Battersea Park Zoo and the ZSL London Zoo in Regent's Park.

Perfect for kids and animal lovers!

## 67. Movie Premieres

The glitzy movie premieres in London always take place in Leicester Square. If you want to star watch, then grab a spot early and wait for the show to begin! Be sure to arrive early as you can expect big crowds.

## 68. National Gallery

Dedicate at least half a day to exploring the National Gallery. It's still won't be enough, but give yourself time to explore the beautiful works of art. We definitely recommend going through with a guidebook or taking the audio tour.

## 69. Tour the BBC

You can tour the working BBC production studios at the BBC Television Centre located in Wood Lane. You can also take a tour of the iconic BBC Broadcasting House in central London.

## 70. Free Museums in London

London is blessed with a world-class selection of museums that have free admission. They often ask for donations, but you can always get in for free. Special exhibitions usually cost money to gain admission.

- British Museum
- National Gallery
- National Portrait Gallery
- Tate Modern
- Tate Britain
- Museum of London
- Docklands Museum
- Natural History Museum
- Science Museum
- Victoria and Albert Museum
- Bank of London Museum
- Imperial War Museum
- London Political Cartoon Gallery
- Museum of Garden History
- National Maritime Museum
- Petrie Museum of Egyptian Archaeology
- RIBA Architecture Gallery
- Sir John Soane's Museum

## 71. Five Things to Do in the East End

The East End of London has a chequered reputation as a rougher area, but that's changing very quickly with the Olympics taking place in summer 2012. Here are our five things not to miss in the East End.

**Westfield Stratford City** - The largest shopping mall in Europe.

**Brick Lane Market** - A diverse and vibrant market not to miss!

**Museum in the Docklands** - Explore London's maritime history at this free museum.

**The Geffrye Museum** - See how London families lived through the centuries.

**Whitechapel Gallery** - Wonderful art gallery.

## 72. Five Things to Do in Shepherd's Bush

Shepherd's Bush isn't really on London's tourist trail, but it's one of our favorite areas of London because it's a very "lived in" place. Here are a few things you can do in the area.

**Westfield London** - Westfield's other giant London mall.

**BBC Television Centre** - They offer daily tours behind the scenes at BBC headquarters.

**Shepherd's Bush Market** - Quirky market open daily.

**K West Hotel & Spa** - If you're in need of a spa day while in London, this is the place to go.

**Shepherd's Bush Vue** - Modern multiplex movie theatre that will be less crowded than theatres in the West End.

# Chapter 6
# SHOPPING

Shopping is one of our favorite things to do when we're in London. Here are a few things that we've learned over the years.

## 73. Five Places to Shop

We have a few favorite places we like to visit while we're in town. We try to avoid places where we can shop back home as they all have the same products these days. We like to hit chains that aren't in the USA and local stores you won't find anywhere else.

**Oxford Street** - This is tourist alley, but you'll find all the major British brands as well as big department stores. It will also be very busy.

**New Bond Street (pricey)** - Home to a series of pricey boutiques where it's fun to window shop.

**Westfield Malls** - London is now home to two mega Westfield Shopping Malls. There are two locations: White City/Shepherds Bush near the BBC Headquarters and the other is in Stratford City (where the Olympics are being held), which is Europe's largest mall.

**Camden Lock Market** - This market is for young people and will feature the latest urban designs and young designers. It's a bustling market that sprawls over several areas that all have their own distinct feel. Also a great place to eat!

**Portobello Road Market** - This market is now pretty much geared toward tourists seeking to relive the film Notting Hill. When it takes place on Saturdays, it will be mobbed with tourists, almost to point where it's hard to walk down the street. That said, it's a fun experience the first time as you find all kinds of cool stuff you won't find anywhere else. Don't expect to find any deals though – it's tourist priced.

## 74. Fashion Central

Because it's in Europe, London gets new fashions first before they catch on in America. Girls, take note of what Londonistas are wearing, as the styles will make it to America in the coming months.

Check out the local Topshops, Zaras, and FCUKs for the latest fashions that you can export back home. You'll be on the cutting edge of the latest fashion trends.

## 75. Used Books on the Thames

There's a great used book market located under Waterloo Bridge on the Southbank of the Thames. It's open daily, and we've always found a good selection of books – some that you won't find in the USA. Many of the books have knockdown prices. There's nothing like browsing amongst old books on the banks of the Thames.

## 76. Where to Find More Books in London

Charing Cross Road is legendary for its array of musty old bookstores. Sadly, many have not survived into the 20th Century. But there are still a lot of great used and niche bookstores clustered on Charing Cross Road near Leicester Square.

Here's a list of 6 bookstores worth visiting.

1. Gosh! Comic Book store in Soho

2. Foyle's Books - One of the best bookstores in London

3. Books and Comic Exchange in Notting Hill

4. Forbidden Planet - Geek haven in Central London on Shaftesbury Avenue.

5. Partners & Crime Mystery Bookstore

6. Hathard's of Piccadilly – The oldest bookstore in London.

## 77. Harrods Tips

Harrods almost deserves its own dedicated day in any London itinerary. Here are a few tips to make the most of your time in the world's most famous department store.

Harrods has different hours on Sunday (they used to just be closed). They are open 11:30 am – 6 pm on Sunday.

Their regular hours are Mon-Sat 10 am – 9 pm.

There is a variety of places to eat in Harrods, including sushi, tea, sandwich shops, and more.

There is a dress code. You must look clean and presentable or they may not let you in (they didn't let Madonna in once!). No torn jeans, sweatpants, etc. Their website has more details.

You need to pay before you leave a particular department. It may be one big store, but it's more like a mall with separate shops.

There's a Harrods shop at the airport that will have most of the major souvenirs, and it will be tax-free there.

If you spend £100 or more you can claim back your VAT on the spot (20% of your purchase!). Big savings!

They will let you pay in US dollars at the till, but we do not recommend doing so as you will not get the best exchange rate. Best to pay in cash or credit card in pounds sterling.

## 78. Five Very Old Stores

London is one of the oldest cities on the planet, and there are several stores that have been operating for many hundreds of years. Here's a quick list of a few worth visiting.

- Twinings Tea Store since 1717 - The original home for Twinings Tea.

- Lock & Co Hatters since 1676 - They sell the best English-style hats money can buy (with a price to match!).

- James Smith & Sons since 1830 - They make and sell custom umbrellas and have a fun store to browse.

- The Old Curiosity Shop since 1666 - They sell curiosities and are famous for their connection to the Dickens story.

- Hamley's Toy Store since 1760 - London's toy mecca. Must see if you have children.

- Hacthards of Piccadilly - Oldest bookstore in London since 1858.

## 79. Top Five Things to See and Do in Bloomsbury

This genteel and quiet area of London is home to world-class museums and famous for its literary connections.

**British Museum** - No trip to London is complete without a visit to the British Museum. GIve yourself plenty of time to explore.

**Russell Square** - Relax amongst the giant old trees in our favorite London Square.

**Cartoon Museum** - See the history of the art behind cartooning.

**British Library** - Britain's national library. Don't miss the Magna Carta.

**Senate House** - Stunning art-deco architecture at the University of London.

## 80. Top Five Things to See and Do on the Southbank

The South Bank of the River Thames is a vibrant and fun area to spend time. It's one of our favorite places in London. Here are five things we love to do.

**London Eye** - A must for any first-time visitor to London. It will help orient you geographically. You really only need to do it once, though.

**Tate Modern** - We're more into the building itself than the art inside, but worth a visit.

**Imperial War Museum** - Dedicated to Britain's Empire and the wars it fought. Not to be missed.

**National Theatre** - Take in a show at the recently renovated National Theatre.

**Globe Theatre** - Take a tour of the reconstructed Globe Theatre, and stay for a play.

# Chapter 7

# HEALTH & SAFTEFY

This section will fill you in on a few ways to stay healthy and safe while you travel in London.

## 81. London is Smoke-Free!

There is pretty much no smoking anywhere in London, including pubs. The days of the smoky pub are now extinct.

It's great - you no longer have to sit in the smoking/non-smoking section, and places like Gordon's Wine Bar are no longer so smoky it's uncomfortable.

## 82. Watch out for Pickpockets!

I know that sounds like travel advice from the 1880s, but believe it or not, they are everywhere, and they prey on American tourists (who are easily identified).

Don't carry all your money with you or your passport. Keep ID and money in a buttoned pocket or a pocket with Velcro so you'll notice if someone tries to pickpocket you.

We've been pickpocketed (thankfully there was nothing for them to steal!), and it's not a pleasant experience. The thieves are usually gone right after you realize you were just pickpocketed.

## 83. Public Toilets

London is home to a ton of free and paid public toilets. Many businesses don't have toilets accessible to the public (which is considered a right in the USA), so the city makes up for it by providing facilities throughout the capital.

They're obviously a useful convenience when you're "caught short" (as the British say). Some are free to use, and others charge a fee. Paying to use a public toilet is rather a strange concept for Americans to get, but once you realize it pays for security and cleanliness, it's worth the few pence you have to pay.

Keep in mind, though, that the free public toilets will be magnets for less than savory characters, especially at night in places like Leicester Square. We've been scared to death by drug addicts and crazies on several journeys around London at night. We recommend avoiding the public conveniences at night.

## 84. National Health Service for Tourists

Yes, the UK has free healthcare. However, foreigners traveling in the UK don't have unlimited access to it. If you have an emergency, you don't have to worry about paying a bill. If you require longer care, they can and will bill you. It's a good idea to take out travel insurance if you're worried about your health while abroad. Travel Insurance will help ensure you get all the care you would require.

Do not be afraid to go to a British hospital if you have an emergency. You will get treated with the same quality of care you would get back home.

They call their emergency rooms "Accident & Emergency" – often just shortened to A&E (not the TV channel).

If you have a medical emergency, dial 999 – that's the British version of 911.

## 85. Pharmacy as a Resource

If you have a minor ailment, visit the local pharmacy. They are operated a little differently from pharmacies in the USA. Pharmacists in the UK have more medial training and can recommend more treatments for various ailments.

When Mrs. Anglotopia was pregnant on one of our trips a few years ago, the travel made her very ill. She went into a pharmacy, and they gave her invaluable advice that put her in much better shape, and let us enjoy the rest of our trip.

Also note that pharmacists in the UK are called chemists. It's also a good idea to take any over the counter medicines you need with you on the trip as they may not be available in Britain or have different names.

## 86. Areas to Avoid

Be cautious in the following areas, as they aren't exactly tourist friendly.

**Earl's Court** - It's improving and there are a lot of cheap hotels there, but it's still rough.

**East London** - While this area is improving thanks to preparations for the Olympics, stay away from housing projects and similar dodgy areas.

**Soho** – It can be a little scary after dark, so be on guard.

**Brixton** - Still pretty rough.

**Notting Hill Estates** - A stone's throw from Portobello Road market are some pretty dodgy housing estates (aka housing projects).

## 87. Lost Property Office

Loss happens. We've lost quite a few things on London's Transport Network on our travels. Thankfully, nothing we missed. However, if you do lose something valuable on the Tube, the Bus or in a London taxi, it will most likely get turned over to the Transport For London Lost Property Office.

Located next to the Baker Street Tube Station, the Lost Property Office manages the over 184,000 lost items left in their care. If you lose something, contact them right away so they can see if they found it, or add you to their system so you're notified when it turns up.

# Chapter 8

# TRANSPORT

This handy chapter will help you make the most of London's transport network and ensure that you travel smoothly throughout London.

## 88. Get an Oyster Card

An Oyster Card is a electronic card used across the Tube network in London and also some National Rail trains. You swipe it to get through the gates at any station. It's a much quicker way to travel across the network, and it's very popular.

It's popular because you always get the lowest fare possible when you use it. If you use the Tube several times during the day, you won't pay more than a certain price for your entire day of journeys. Use of the Oyster card is also heavily discounted – you save over 50% versus paying cash for a ticket.

Before you leave for London, buy an Oyster card for the London Underground as they get the cheapest fare. It's much cheaper than buying a day or week pass. You can purchase them easily from Visit Britain Direct You can also purchase one while you're in London, but it's easier to buy it before you get there.

## 89. London Transport Operating Hours

The Tube Closes after midnight and opens around 5 am depending on the line. If you plan to be out late, you'll need to rely on London Black Taxis or the bus to get back to your hotel.

The bus system runs 24 hours, so you can always rely on that to get where you need to go. Buses are also cheaper than the Tube, and you'll get more local this way.

You can expect London Black Taxis to operate through the night, but they will become harder to find the later (and earlier) it gets. Avoid minicabs at all costs as they are unlicensed and don't require the training that Black Cab drivers have. We've also had strange experiences when looking for a cab where random people will offer us a ride. Don't ever do this.

## 90. Tube Geography

Leicester Square Tube Stop and Covent Garden Tube Stop are literally several hundred feet from each other, but Leicester Square can handle the crowds better.

If you want to go to Covent Garden, get off at Leicester Square, and walk up Longacre to Covent Garden. There will be signs to direct you.

Covent Garden Tube has very slow elevators, and the crowds build up very quickly in this popular tourist area. There are too many stairs to climb (the signs tell you this).

## 91. Getting from the Airports to London

The Heathrow Express to London Paddington Station is the quickest and easiest way to get into central London from the airport. It's a bit pricey, but it's quiet and a nice ride after a long flight. It drops you right in the middle of everything, and it's easy to get transport to your hotel from Paddington.

The Gatwick Express operates similarly to the Heathrow Express, but it takes a little longer as Gatwick is further away from London.

The Tube is the cheapest way to get to London from Heathrow, but takes three times as long as it has to make all the stops.

We would avoid taking a cab from the airport, as you'll spend about $100 on cab fare – money much better spent on your entertainment in London itself rather than getting there.

## 92. Getting to Paris

High Speed trains to Paris depart from St. Pancras station now, and it takes just 2:15 minutes to get there. If you're this close, why not go for the day? It will be worth it.

A day trip to Paris is a great way to experience the city but not have to stay there. You can see most of the major sites, have a dinner at a café, and be back in London in time for bedtime.

A Eurostar ticket will cost you about $100 and is well worth the money. Don't even think about flying from London to Paris. It's just not that far, and you'll spend a fortune getting from Paris's airport to central Paris. The Eurostar drops you right in the middle of Paris.

## 93. Five London Taxi Etiquette Tips

Riding in a London Black Taxi is an experience that every tourist much do. While taking a taxi will be more expensive than other transport options, it's truly a London experience. Cabbies are usually very friendly and happy to have a conversation with you. Marvel at the turning radius of a taxi.

1. Like in most cities, the taxi's light on top of the cab must be on. The light signals that the taxicab can be hired.

2. Wave to hail a cab. Don't yell, "Taxi!".

3. It's polite procedure to ask the cabbie if he can take you where you want to go BEFORE you get in the cab.

4. They won't mind being tipped, but it's okay not to tip them or just round up to the nearest pound.

5. Avoid minicabs as they are unlicensed and don't require the thorough training that Black Cab drivers must have.

## 94. Rush Hour on the Tube

It's best to just avoid the Tube at rush hour. You'll just annoy everyone trying to get to work or home. Morning rush hour is over after 9 am, and evening rush hour is between 4 and 6 pm.

The Tube is very crowded during rush hour and is doing what it was designed to do – taking Londoners from home to work and vice versa. If you choose to travel during rush hour, be prepared for a crush.

## 95. Ten Tube Etiquette Tips

Here are a few tips to behave properly on the Tube so your trip goes as smoothly as possible.

1. Never talk to anyone other than your own party, and even that will be frowned upon. If you must talk, do so quietly.

2. Give up your seat for an old or pregnant person.

3. Though it is quite tempting, don't read over other people's shoulders.

4. Let passengers off the train before trying to get on.

5. Your bag or suitcase is not entitled to a seat, especially if the train is crowded.

6. Stand on the right on escalators

7. Wear deodorant or cologne. Please.

8. Always have your Oyster Card or ticket ready.

9. Don't eat on the train.

10. Watch out for pickpockets. They work the Tube system.

## 96. Heated Tubes

The London Underground gets REALLY hot in the summer, so plan accordingly. Always have a bottle of water to stay cool.

## 97. Going through Customs on Arrival

If you've never gone through arrival customs before, don't be too afraid. It's no sweat and can be kind of fun.

On the plane they will give you a landing card. Follow the directions carefully. If it's not filled out properly, you'll have to fill it out again in Customs (holding up the line).

When you get off the plan, I recommend doing your best powerwalk so you get to the front of the line.

There is no special line for Americans. You're in the queue with the rest of the world. It's rather humbling.

Answer the customs agent's questions honestly, and give them the landing card.

They'll stamp you in and give you back your passport.

If you have anything to declare (i.e. items you're bringing into the country), you MUST declare it before exiting the customs area.

Welcome to Britain!

## 98. Going Through Customs When Leaving

It's much more straightforward leaving. You don't go through immigration, and you don't have your passport stamped on the way out of the country.

Check in with your airline.

Go through security. It's always wise to wear slip-on shoes.

That's it.

If you saved your receipts and have all your purchases with you, you can claim your VAT back in the terminal.

## 99. What to Do if Your Luggage is Lost

You haven't become a seasoned traveler until your luggage has been lost. Our bags were lost on our second trip to Britain, and that was a fun experience! There's nothing worse than the sick feeling you get as all the luggage is reclaimed from the carousel and yours is nowhere to be found. Here are a few tips for how to deal with the situation.

Stay Calm - Customer service is different – more civil and they won't respond to confrontation.

There's a customer service desk for your airline in the baggage area.

Make your lost claim.

They'll attempt to find it. It's all computerized now, so they'll have some idea where the bag is.

If your bag is found, the airline will deliver it to your hotel at no extra charge.

If it's lost for good, you can make a compensation claim (but this will not help you now).

Also, when packing and if you're going with someone, always put clothes in each other's bags. That way if one of the bags is lost, you'll at least have something to wear when you arrive. It's also a good idea to have a change of clothes in your carry-on. We didn't, and had to buy changes of clothes when we got into London.

## 100. Lost? Need Guidance?

Pop into the Britain and London Tourist Information Centre located right in central London on Regent Street. They'll offer free help and guidance for all your London questions. They'll help you book hotels, theatre tickets, train tickets, etc. They have ample free maps and brochures for the taking. It's an invaluable London resource.

## 101. Think of the Future

You will not have enough time to do everything you want to do in London in one trip. Don't even try. We've been to London 10 times now, and we still can't see everything we want to see.

There's nothing worse than spending your vacation completely exhausted because you're trying to do it all.

Don't stress, manage your time well, understand that it's a foreign place, and you'll have a fantastic time and want to return time and time again. Many people think that they only have one chance to go to London. If you've been once, you can most certainly go again.

Happy London Travels!

# Appendix 1

## 101 Free Things to do in London

1. **British Museum** - The best Museum in London. Plan a whole day here.
2. **National Gallery** – Some of history's best art for free.
3. **Trafalgar Square** – Go see Nelson and people-watch as London goes by.
4. **Walk through Hyde Park** - No trip to London is complete without a walk through Hyde Park.
5. **Covent Garden** – Explore the old market, watch street performers, hear musicians. Plenty of free fun to be had in Covent Garden!
6. **Walk along the Thames** – Smell the fresh river air and listen to the Thames lap along the shore.
7. **Tate Modern** – Some of the art is questionable, but the building is amazing in itself and worth a visit alone.
8. **Evensong Church Service** – You have to pay admission to get into most of London's cathedrals, but if you go to evensong service you can get in for free.
9. **Cross Tower Bridge** - It's a free thrill for all tourists to cross the bridge! Wait around, and you might even see it open and close.
10. **National Maritime Museum** – Explore Britain Royal Navy's history.

11. **Walk through the Woolwich Foot Tunnel** – Cross one of the oldest tunnels under the Thames – get off a the DLR stop King George V and walk to the entrance.
12. **Pollocks Toy Museum** – Toys from around the world – great place for the kids!
13. **Imperial War Museum** – See Britain's Military History in all its glory.
14. **Borough Market** – Explore one of London's coolest markets!
15. **British Film Institute's Mediatheque** – Explore Britain's film heritage.
16. **Houses of Parliament** - It costs money to go inside, but that doesn't have to stop you from checking out the building from the outside.
17. **Museum of London** – Fun look at the history of London.
18. **National Portrait Gallery** – Might not interest everyone as it's pictures of aristocracy through the ages.
19. **Natural History Museum** – One of the world's finest natural history museums. Check out the Darwin Centre!
20. **Victoria and Albert Museum** – A strange hodge-podge museum that provides an interesting insight into Britain's cultural heritage.
21. **Science Museum** – Who doesn't like science? Kids will love it!

22. **Serpentine Gallery** – Art Gallery located in Hyde Park that rotates various exhibitions through the year.
23. **Tate Britain** - Like the National Gallery, it's home to some beautiful art.
24. **Guildhall Art Gallery** – Collection of art collected by the Corporation of London.
25. **Wallace Collection** – Collection of European art and artifacts.
26. **Whitechapel Gallery** – Modern Art gallery in East London.
27. **Bank of England Museum** – Take a look at the monetary history of the world.
28. **Changing of the Guard** – It's a tourist trap, but always fun to see on a sunny day. Every day in the summer at 11:30. Arrive early.
29. **Ceremony of the Keys** - You have to request permission to witness this, but it's pretty cool. Watch the nightly lock-up of the Tower of London.
30. **Sir John Soane's Museum** – The eclectic collection of a famous London architect exactly as he left it.
31. **Kenwood House** – Lovely stately home located in Hampstead Heath.
32. **Geffrye Museum** – Period rooms museum from 1600 to today.
33. **Royal Air Force Museum** – See the history of Britain's flying aces.
34. **Horniman Museum** – An eclectic family museum with many different displays.

35. **Queen Mary's Rose Garden** - London's largest and best rose garden.
36. **St James' Park** – One of London's fine Royal Parks.
37. **The Globe Theatre** – See the replica of the theatre that was home to Shakespeare's plays! It costs to get in for a tour, but not to have a look outside.
38. **Princess Diana Memorial** - Located in Hyde Park, you can pay your respects to Princess Di.
39. **Speaker's Corner** - Arrive on a Sunday morning, and watch the colorful characters gathered to speak about anything.
40. **Leicester Square** – Relax in the park in the middle or admire the glitzy lights of this tourist haven.
41. **Tower Bridge Lifts** – Watch Tower Bridge open and close.
42. **Museum of London Docklands** - A lesser known London, but cool none the less. You can explore London's maritime shipping history.
43. **Lunch Concerts at St. Martin in the Fields** – Enjoy lunch in the Crypt at St. Martin in the Fields, and also enjoy free concerts every day.
44. **Free Concerts at the National Theatre** – Check with them for regular free concerts open to the public.

45. **Watch a TV Show Recorded at the BBC** – It's free to be in the studio audience of a show as it's being recorded.
46. **View London from Primrose Hill** – Admire the view from London's Primrose Hill.
47. **London Silver Vaults** - Check out the world's largest retail collection of fine antique silver.
48. **Hunterian Museum** – See a unique collection of animal specimens kept in jars.
49. **Watch a Trial at Central Criminal Court** – It's free to watch a trial take place from the public galleries at the Central Criminal Court.
50. **Walk through the City on a Saturday** – The Square Mile or City of London is practically abandoned on the weekends. Check out the cool architecture and enjoy the quiet streets.
51. **Street Performers in Covent Garden or the South Bank** – Seek out buskers throughout London for free and fun entertainment.
52. **Catch a Film Premiere in Leicester Square** – The Odeon Theatre in Leicester Square regularly holds film premieres where you can catch a glimpse of stars.
53. **Coram's Fields** - Unique seven-acre playground and park for children living in or visiting London.
54. **Foundling Museum** - Britain's original home for abandoned children and London's first ever public art gallery.

55. **The Photographer's Gallery** – Largest public display gallery dedicated to photography.
56. **Peter Pan Statue** – Check out the statue of the literary classic located in Kensington Gardens.
57. **Museum of Childhood** – Dedicated to the history of childhood.
58. **See the London Stone** – Check out the Roman Stone from where all distance from London was measured located at 111 Cannon Street.
59. **Touch the Roman Wall** – Throughout the city of London you'll see traces of the original Roman Wall fortification. There's large pieces around the Museum of London.
60. **Check out Picadilly Circus** – See the iconic bright lights and the famous statue of Eros.
61. **Musicians in Covent Garden Apple Market** – On the lower levels of the Market, there's usually musicians busking while people eat.
62. **Explore Leadenhall Market** - Gorgeous market located in the City of London worth exploring for the architecture alone.
63. **Walk Across Hampstead Heath** – Beautiful park in London that provides lovely views of metropolitan London.
64. **Visit Regent's Park** – Another great Royal Park, and there's a zoo!

65. **Wellington Arch** – One of two triumphal arches in London.
66. **Marble Arch** – The second triumphal arch in London.
67. **Visit Platform 9 3/4** – Doesn't really exist, of course, but station authorities have set up a fake entrance for Harry Potter fans at King's Cross Station.
68. **Visit St Pancras International** – Admire this beautiful station, watch Eurostar trains arrive and depart, and visit the statue of the couple kissing.
69. **Free Music at the Notting Hill Arts Club** – Regular free music in Notting Hill.
70. **Harrod's Food Hall** – Browse quail eggs, cava, and custom-made cakes in the sumptuous food halls in Harrods.
71. **Walk along the South Bank** – Walk from Waterloo Bridge to the Tate Modern, and see a huge part of London.
72. **Walk through Richmond Park** – Another lovely park.
73. **Changing of the Guard in Windsor** - If you happen to be in Windsor, there's a changing of the guard there as well.
74. **Visit Bushy Park** – Yet another lovely park.
75. **5th View Bar** – Check out the priceless views.
76. **Canals of Maida Vale/Little Venice** – See London's waterways and cute boats where people actually live!

77. **Abbey Road Crosswalk** - Become a traffic hazard, and have your own Beatles pictures taken.

78. **Admire the Barbican** - Built after World War II, it's a triumph of modernism.

79. **Postman's Park** - The square from the movie "Closer" where memorials are dedicated to people who died saving Londoners.

80. **Take a free London guided walk** – Pick up a guidebook or download a free audio tour, and do your own London walk.

81. **Travel Bookshop in Notting Hill** – Visit the bookstore that the shop in the film *Notting Hill* was based on.

82. **Portobello Road Market** – Be prepared for huge crowds, but no visit to London is complete without a visit to the bustling market.

83. **Explore Blue Plaques** - Look closely on old buildings, and you'll see lots of blue plaques, which offer some history about famous people who lived there.

84. **Listen to Big Ben Chime** – Stand in Parliament Square at noon and wait for Big Ben to make its music.

85. **Visit the U.S. Embassy** – You can't go inside unless you have business, but you can admire the building and the beautiful square that surrounds it.

86. **Visit the Cenotaph** – Pay respects to Britain's memorials to the two World Wars.

87. **Explore Camden Town and Camden Lock Market** – Much bigger than Portobello Road and much more to see.
88. **Check out City Hall and the Scoop** - Admire London's new bee-hive-shaped city hall and watch out for free performances in the Scoop outside.
89. **Visit 10 Downing Street** – Get a glimpse of the residence of the Prime Minister. Wait long enough, and you might see him come and go.
90. **Picnic in Battersea Park** – Lovely riverside park with views of the Thames.
91. **Cross the Jubilee Bridge** – Cross the Thames at Embankment on this beautiful bridge.
92. **Cross the Millennium Bridge** – Best way to cross from the Tate Modern to St Paul's or vice verse.
93. **See the Roosevelt & Churchill Statue** - Located in Bond Street, see the two great world leaders as friends.
94. **See the Churchill Statue** – Located in Parliament Square.
95. **See the Lincoln Statue** - Statue of the American president located in Parliament Square. The only one to have such an honor.
96. **Free WiFi in the Apple Stores** – Need wifi or access to the web? Then stop in the Apple Stores in Covent Garden or Regent Street and recharge your Internet batteries.

97. **Get Photographed in a Red Phone Box** – Nothing more touristy or more awesome than a picture in a red phone box.

98. **Visit the National Army Museum** – Discover the history of Britain's armed forces.

99. **Visit Russell Square** – Quiet little green park in the middle of bustling London right around the corner from the British Museum.

100. **Visit the 7-7 Memorial** - Located in Hyde Park on the east side, you can pay your respects to those who lost their lives in the terror attacks on 7-7-05.

101. **Feed the Ducks in St James Park** – They'll appreciate it!

## ABOUT ANGLOTOPIA

Anglotopia.net is the world's largest gathering place for Anglophiles. Founded in 2007 by Jonathan and Jacqueline Thomas as a hobby it grew to become a massive online community of dedicated Anglophiles. Jonathan and Jacqueline now work full time on Anglotopia and its sister websites. They travel to the UK at least once a year to do research.

68673990R00080

Made in the USA
San Bernardino, CA
07 February 2018